Terror of a New Age

Terror of a New Age

◆

A Vivid Glimpse at the State of Humanity in a New Millennium

Cleran Hollancid

…taking a moment to consider the time in which we live

iUniverse, Inc.
New York Lincoln Shanghai

Terror of a New Age
A Vivid Glimpse at the State of Humanity in a New Millennium

iUniverse books may be ordered through booksellers or by contacting:

iUniverse
2021 Pine Lake Road, Suite 100
Lincoln, NE 68512
www.iuniverse.com
1-800-Authors (1-800-288-4677)

ISBN-13: 978-0-595-40997-6 (pbk)
ISBN-13: 978-0-595-85351-9 (ebk)
ISBN-10: 0-595-40997-0 (pbk)
ISBN-10: 0-595-85351-X (ebk)

Printed in the United States of America

Dedicated

To my mother, Eldrina Hollancid, who has undoubtedly touched my life in a profound way. I esteem her highly for her strength of character. I honor her as a most worthy parent, and for being a role model and mentor to others. It is out of my deep gratitude to her, and my appreciation of her, I consider her to be the greatest mother of all times.

Contents

Preface ....*xi*

Our World 1

1 Today's World *3*

2 Mankind's Calamity *11*

The World of 9/11 25

3 Islam at a Glance *27*

4 The Dawn of 9/11 ....*41*

The Post-9/11 World 53

5 *When Tragedy Strikes* 55

6 *The Da Vinci Awakening* 63

7 *Facing the 21st Century* 73

Endnotes 85

Acknowledgements

A special thanks to my wife, Rebecca, for her intent contribution in the manuscript review process; and to a couple of my colleagues for very insightful critiques.

Preface

From 9/11 (2001) to what I call the Da Vinci Awakening (2006), it seems as though people are examining their raison d'etre—a reason for their existence, so to speak. What is life if there are no historical landmarks and telltales? Life, in that sense, is perceived largely from events akin to human interests and passions.

Likewise, enduring socio-political crises and natural disasters on a colossal scale, over the past few years, seem to have built a fusion of resolve and frustration in the human mind. One point that has been reinforced, however, in the past half decade is: give human minds something to live for, and they will attempt to live for it. This half decade (2001-2006) thus marks a new shift in Western (if not human) psyche. A new day has arrived, but is mankind doomed to the folly of the past?

This new paradigm, or shift that I speak of in the opening years of the twenty-first century and a new millennium, marks the dawn of a new age. It tells the story of the mutative, if not transformative, nature of human character. In this mode, however, people are looking for God in all sorts of places, but more so, perhaps within the human experience. In so doing, people are necessarily also getting to know of God through a sort of modern collective social consciousness.

I must say here that this book, though it poses many reflective questions about human society, is not specifically designed to be an answer booklet. Actually, this book is set in such a way as to warrant the inclusion of a broad range of issues. So if you come across gaps that you deem necessary to fill in, that perhaps is not the manifest aim of the book. The objective of this author, rather, is not to pretend to expose, or to have all the solutions to social tensions and global decadence, but to attempt to stimulate reader awareness and think-ing.

Furthermore, this book is not to be taken as a handbook of all crises, or significant events mark-ing the beginning of the twenty-first century. Instead, the material composed herein, draws upon a peculiar perspective, as seen through the eyes of the expositor.

This book, which can be read more as a per-sonal commentary, exhibits observations on con-temporary society. And though it is written with a secular audience in mind, it is actually placed in a general social construct, whereby it can be perused by readers from all walks of life. In that light, it traces some of the crucial events that go along with human transition and adaptation that have, to a great extent, characterized the initial formative years of Western civilization and human life in the twenty-first century.

C. L. Hollancid

Our World

Observation: We are living in a new millennium, yet in a world that is scarred with the folly of the past, and assailed by all sorts of terror in a new and modern age.

1   Today's World

*H*ave you ever given earnest thought to the world in which you live? One may think that life would only get better with all the breakthroughs in health research, space exploration, the establishment of the United Nations—a body designed to keep world peace, and the accommodations of modern technology. Since that does not seem to be the case, we seek to understand the human realm and extract meaning from a world compelled by contradiction, and scarred with conflict.

Here we are in 2006, living in a technological age our forebears could not even imagine. Yet it is an age of intelligence and an age of foolishness; the age of information, but increasingly we struggle with the misappropriation and lack of information; an age of illumination, an age of hopelessness; an age of accomplishment yet an age of wickedness; an age of productivity but an age of horror; an age of establishment yet an age of uncertainty; an age of gain and an age of selfishness; an age of wit, an age of folly; an age of self aggrandizement when the lofty arrogance of men and women fly high in the very face of God.

Everywhere people seem to be going about without direction and sense of purpose. And the more there's talk of peace, the more there seems to be war, discouragement, and an upsurge in calamity on every hand. To be honest, God doesn't seem to play a role in today's modern world, as the heart of mankind is ever moving towards taking personal credit for everything. And many people fail to see any point or design in life, perhaps because life appears to be an endless pain with a painful end.

As in days of old, today there is talk about how malicious and unfriendly the world we live in really is. Many seem to have a challenge in tolerating those who look or think differently from them. Take for instance the subject of Islam (the focus of an upcoming chapter); by and large, the Western mindset appears to be placed at invariable friction with Islamic culture. With all the socio-cultural advancement looming in the face of modern man, we look around and there seems to be a suffusion of hatred, civil unrest, materialism and ungodliness. How does one find their niche in a pessimistic and dissolute world?

The rise in global artillery, war, local and international, confrontational issues; the political

debauchery of the pre-2001 era; the sordid experi-
ences of 2001 and beyond; the endless peace nego-
tiations between Jews and Muslims; the
unrelenting tumult between tribes and nations of
earth; the aftershock of hideous tragedies, and the
heightened secularism that pervades society, all
seem to be steering the tide toward a godless
future.

People are seeking meaning from a nefarious
world, apparently growing colder by the minute.
From the pre-Christian era, to when Christ
walked the earth, to late antiquity, the Middle
Ages, the Renaissance, Enlightenment, modern
and post-modern eras, various societies have
relentlessly tried to leave their mark on history at

the expense of staying the tide of inter-cultural apathy and antagonism. Yet, people are always attempting to extract meaning from contemporary events and interpret the circumstances surrounding their lives, in an effort to fathom the delirious world around them.

In that vein, for the most part, as far as we can assess the history of man, war seems to be a key player and a perennial theme that characterizes major stages of earth's sociological development. Prehistoric, historic, and current times all divulge the ambitions of rulers and armies to imprint their identity on the world's stage, through the instrument of warfare. And where has it led to?

Apparently, some rulers, governments and princes get sold out on the doctrine that promulgates the impression, "if there is no contention and war, there is no life." From America to Africa to Afghanistan to Cambodia—no region appears immune to the damnable disease. So many wars and civil strife have blotched the highway of human history, that it seems virtually impossible to study the history of war and adequately chronicle, or cover the full saga. It's all a power struggle which, many a time, seems to characterize the avaricious appetite of the ruling class. Human society is then left to reckon with the ravages and consequences of political superfluity.

But what of mankind—can they help it? What is mankind's plight? We resume this discourse with our attention on the state of man in a corroded sphere.

2 Mankind's Calamity

*W*e are all participants currently fastened inside cosmic struggle, much of which seems to be social and spiritual. It behooves one, therefore, to ponder exactly what is the object of life? As teleological (or purposeful) beings, then, we come face to face not only with the whole notion of human frailty and instability, but human endeavor as well.

As we take a good look at the state of our world today, however, we see that society languishes and is destitute for solutions to the problems of war, diseases, heartaches, poverty, greed, divorce, personal troubles, and moral decadence. It appears that the more committee meetings, government summits and peace talks transpire, the more bloodshed, greed and arrogance intensify. Then we see that while some are living in what one might consider comfort zones—have food to eat, clothes to wear, shelter, and so on, others face anguish—struggling to get perhaps even a morsel of rice per day, if so much; having to watch their family being murdered in cold blood, hustling to the nearest asylum for protection of life, and so forth.

All these altercations and grievances are also fueled by bigotry, racism, ethnic tension and prejudice all over the world. They indubitably cling onto a rapid downward ride to the putrefied stench of the corruption of human attitude and behavior. To top it off, men and women continue to take a stand against any notion of the supernatural.

In that vein, ideologies such as naturalism, macro-evolution, and humanism have besieged social consciousness. What does that mean? I'm glad you asked. As the situation goes, the changing sentiments of the time, from around the seventeenth to nineteenth century, led to a new influx of philosophical thought. This particularly caught sway in regions such as Europe and North America. Some refer to the period as being a time of enlightenment. Men like James Hutton and Charles Lyell came on the scene with a new view of the world—naturalism.

And the mood surrounding such a climate?—in the late eighteenth century, France experienced the traumatic French Revolution, leading to a reconstruction in socio-political values, which eventually spread beyond the borders of France. Germany, around that time to the nineteenth century, in a sense, piloted a sort of religio-intel-lectual transformation, featuring guys like Friedrich Schleiermacher and Albrecht Ritschl. And England spearheaded the industrial revolution (in that same milieu), with London rising up as the financial hub of the world.[1]

Alongside that, a class struggle persisted in the middle of the 19th century. Due to laissez faire ideas of capitalism, laborers and the lower social classes were being economically squeezed, with relatively very few people being actual wealthy property owners. The labor situation proved to be a huge disaster, with child labor and very long work days being top concerns.

At that time there was no real bargaining power, or even the slightest notion of a labor union for the average citizen. Hence, it isn't baffling to sense how exploitation and disenfranchisement became rampant. It is indeed out of that climate, another modern socio-challenge began to take root in Europe. Thus, in 1848, that particular season of unbalanced profits in the classification of labor, ushered in a popular book: the *Communist Manifesto*, published by, Friedrich Engels and Karl Marx.[2] It is precisely in light of this era of change, that the ideas of naturalism started to gain momentum in England and elsewhere.

According to naturalist (philosophical) ideas, the earth was considered to have developed through natural causes, rather than supernatural. Thus, in the mid-nineteenth century, there was a sudden thrust to shift the emphasis and mankind's objective point of reference, from the supernatural to the natural. Such a daring move, as you may be aware, progressed and was applied to not only geological studies, but also to the study of organisms and species—all life forms.

The stage was set for the modern views of macro-evolution and natural selection (the process of modifications of species, through extensive time and variable scheme of descent). It is not without curiosity then, that many started to view the works of Charles R. Darwin, especially his piece, "Origin of Species" coming out in the late

1850s. In other words, this humanistic (system of human-centric values and thought) approach to the world, created a whole new wave of thinking. This, no doubt, constituted a distinct transition in human restlessness. For many, this eventually translated to—God simply doesn't exist.

Does the idea of a supernatural being overseeing you, raise any inkling of reverence? Well in today's society, God is dead. More than ever before, it appears that the world is in a determined fight to dethrone the Ruler of the universe. That this is the case, seems to be evident in many spiritual sways, and also among some who claim to have so-called scientific, theosophical and anthroposophical knowledge. The landscape of our current age endorses the motif of looking inward (to the self) for energy and guidance. Forget God.

The funny thing is, the more people try to disprove that God exists, the more they inadvertently produce the opposing effect. I will just illustrate this from one of the many angles with which you can approach the subject.

I would like to introduce what I consider to be the 'theory of epistematics,' a term I coined to deal with the origin of knowledge. The term comes from the Greek word, *episteme*—meaning: 'know, knowing, knowledge.' In its prime definition, this personal theory states that—the knowable is already known.

Hence, in essence, this presupposes that one of the ways in which human growth takes place is to simply discover what's already known. Think of it as a body of knowledge which mankind digs from to gain knowledge that also stimulates human thinking. In other words, one cannot learn if there's absolutely nothing to learn about; and where did the information for learning and knowledge come from in the first place?—certainly not within the realm of human ingenuity. Thus, there's just no way of getting around it; humans are finite drawing from the infinite.

Humans also seem to be in a frenzy seeking to establishing solidarity, by and among themselves, in a world that many a time seems to have nothing to offer. In the midst of such darkness, fear grips the human spirit as from newsflash to newsflash humans wonder what will happen next! It's no wonder why, then, that it may now seem more of a delusion to think of world peace. Besides, societies all over the world are unstable and live in constant fear of the uncertainties of tomorrow—fear of failure, fear of death and everything else in between.

Humanity is constantly seeking freedom and tranquility that appear to be slipping away like sand in the hourglass. The hour has come for men and women to consider their ways. You can almost hear one human calling to another, as the great quest for a solution to sheer depravity and glaring pessimism continues to paint a dismal picture for the order of current existence.

Mankind's fear of the troubles that threaten and degrade the human domain, is further exacerbated by political squabbles, sending victims to an ominous grave all across this suicidal and blood-paved planet. Mankind has literally been thrown into the realm of destitution. This I refer to as, '**The Great Socio-Indicative Crisis,**' that is bringing the world to its knees.

As narcissism and tidings of strife continue to ravage modern society in the 21st century, and pull behind it a weight of socio-economic hardship, the blackened skies continue to spell rebellion and restlessness for earth's masses. Through all this, some of the rich are getting stouter, while the poor are left to drink their own blood. But now there's a new buzz word in town—*terrorism*. Not that the idea of hostile attacks between communities and ethnic groups is anything new, but in today's society it is taking on the size of an international action field, with sides pitted against each other. And so today, in the West for instance, there is much talk of terrorism and Islam. In order to get a better grip on the whole affair, however, one has to take a closer look at the meaning of Islam.

The World of 9/11

Observation: At the opening of the 21st century there was no arousing universal movement to awaken the nerve of global rally. But on 9/11/2001 the world changed.

3   Islam at a Glance

*T*he rise in Islamic consciousness, one might say, left a dauntless and pervasive mark on modern culture and the western mind in the 20th century. Born and bred in Middle-eastern culture, Islam is viewed with perennial aberration and strangeness by many in the western world. And some even tend to view the world through their personal lens of Christianity vs. Islam. But besides that, many understand Islam as being peppered with chronic political agitation and social strife.

In the last century, Islamic beliefs and culture perhaps would not have been a notable topic in the West, in terms of a relatively widespread pre-occupation with, and concern for, the subject had it not been for political crises in the Middle East. This indirectly affected major world players, such as America, Russia, France and England.

In modern times, war and civil strife on the rise related to the Middle East, has been a growing motif in media broadcasts. Events such as the fight for Israel's nationhood and recognition in the 1940's, the Arab-Israeli Suez Crisis of 1956, the Six-day War of 1967—Israel versus Egypt, Syria and Jordan, the Afghan-Soviet War—1979-1989, the eight-year Iran-Iraq War of the 1980's, the Persian Gulf War at the opening of the last decade of the 20th century, and the 9/11 event, all attracted the attention of the public.

Such unremitting aggression and bloody feuds certainly leave a distinct impression in the annals of human history. I even heard a song growing up, with lyrics telling of "Rambo Diplomacy," referring to the incessancy of conflict and war in the period of the late 20th century. With all of this warmongering connected in one way or the other to Islamic culture (or Arab politics), Western consciousness was, no doubt, left to reckon with an understanding of Islam.

The question that still begs though is, 'what is Islam?' Is that all there is to Islam—skirmishes and battles? It would certainly be naïve to believe that this is the sum-total of Islam. In Islam, you have the bad and ugly, but there are also the kind-hearted and hopeful.

The term 'Islam,' by and large refers to the civilization of the Muslim world;[3] or the religio-political order supposedly, centrically formed around the life of a man who some recognize by the name, Muhammad ibn Abdullah, "born in Mecca around the year [A.D.] 570...."[4] The word *Islam* itself, is from the Semitic root—*slm*, or a constituent linguistic subgroup that hails from the larger Afro-Asiatic language group. In certain variations *Islam* can be seen as meaning: the act of making peace/be complete, from *aslem* in Syriac; to surrender, from *aslama* in Arabic;[5] and peace, as in *shalom* in the Hebrew.

The name *Muslim,* in this discussion, refers to a follower of the ways of Islam. And *Islam* is characterized as a way of life; in this case, and perhaps more in the socio-religious sense—the way of *submission.* Since I do not propose to go into a lengthy discussion on Islam in this book, suffice it to say that a Muslim is welded, so to speak, to not only religious beliefs as some may think, but also to a particular socio-cultural climate, which engenders politics in many respects; to this last point I will return in a moment.

Islam, in its origins, and certainly within certain cultures today, can also be seen as being communal (as opposed to being individualistic) in nature. Such may be seen in regions of North Africa, the Middle East and Central Asia. Thus, culturally speaking, one may find a Muslim speaking in terms of a community rather than each one for his/her own.

Much, but by no means all, of the Muslim world is Arab, or speaks Arabic. Arabic just happens to be the language in which the world of Islam took root. And hence, the Qur'an—a book which Muslims regard as containing their sacred recordings, is written in Arabic. Many would like to believe that the Qur'an is so sacred and contains God's revelation verbatim, that it must not be translated into any other language. As a matter of fact though, it has been translated into other languages, as Islam sought to expand its original territories.

Though Islam arose from a sort of polytheistic, Arabic culture and claims monotheism for itself, it is riddled with multiple denominations or sects. In a dynamic way much of these sects fall under two wings—Shi'ah and Sunni, with respect to orthodox Islam. Generally speaking, on the one hand, Shi'ites hold dear to the idea of the successive leaders of Islam, following the death of Muhammad, as being more filial in nature. Accordingly, this leadership flows directly from Ali's (Muhammad's son-in-law) line. Each leader (who some may refer to as, *Imam)* should be the one to appoint the next successive leader of the community. On the other hand, Sunni Muslims see leadership (or caliphate) of Islam as not necessarily stemming from a direct descendant of Muhammad. This major division is supposedly the root cause of much of the rivalry and carnage among Muslims. Today, however, Islam has spanned much of the globe, claiming over seven hundred million adherents, with perhaps approximately one percent of them living in the US.

We return now to the idea of Islam also engendering politics in some way. That is not to say that all countries with a dominant Islamic population, are necessarily governed in an Islamic way, or practice Shari'ah law—the religio-cultural, legal code which many Muslims recognize as containing the governing policies of a society. Turkey, though seen as being an Islamic country, for instance, has a rather secular form of government.

The idea of having a secular government oversee an Islamic country has, no doubt, paved the way for more schism within Islam itself. Another issue, in that respect, one has to take into account is that perhaps as early as the sixteenth century, European nations such as, England, France and Holland, assigned themselves the zealous task of colonizing, or annexing a large portion of the world. This did not exclude much of Africa and the Middle East.

Middle Eastern countries, however, fought for and gained their independence around the early to mid-twentieth century. But sooner or later, it became evident that deciding which form of government was to rule the newly independent states, was not going to be a simple walk in the park. Muslims were divided over whether or not to keep Western political influence as the dominant form of government, or to manage their countries purely from an Islamic orientation. For these very reasons, new splinter groups arose in the Middle East to combat, as they see it, the infidel way to run an Islamic country. And so a new cause arose.

It is out of such fever that, what we know as, 'Radical Islam' took on fresh meaning; and with that, the call for arms. Mind you, those who use arms do not represent Islam as a whole, but merely a fraction of separatist movements within Islam. In that vein, another idea which took on new meaning is what we refer to as *jihad*.

Jihad, which really embodies the idea of 'striving,' took on its own new twist within the framework of Islamic radicalism. In that sense, those who take part in jihad as a holy war are sending (in my words) the message—"we are fighting anyone who stands in the way of, or is oppressing the true way of Islam." Thus, we can surmise that the radical arm of Islam also extended its focus and concerns toward the United States, perhaps because of America's fair share of influence in Middle Eastern politics, in the twentieth century and beyond.

This takes us to 9/11. Extremist, or radical groups within Islam are believed to be responsible for the 2001 attacks on US soil, including the assault on the World Trade Center. Since this issue, however, is already divulged ad nauseam, this book does not seek to compose a repeat. But what I can tell you is that the socio-political land-scape of America, and markedly the modern world, generally have been, in one way or the other, affected since 9/11/2001. This date, then, is unmistakably a major watershed in our era of human history. We sustain this discourse as we revisit the agitation of 9/11 for a moment.

4   The Dawn of 9/11

Have you ever dialed the emergency number: 911? If you did, you may recall the rush of anxiety and, perhaps, panic that accompanied the call. That's ok, for all of us find ourselves in distressing situations. But does God have a need to place an emergency call on human lines, or to just contact us? What was it like on 9/11?

On hindsight, mankind looks with horror on the scene. It was a day that would compel the human race to revisit the fragility and vulnerability of human existence, flagitiousness and stealth. Some observed the brunt of the events of September 11, 2001 with awe, while others may have viewed it with much uneasiness. Some even look on this watershed event as a pronounced waymark, telling that the end is near.

For many it was a time of reflection. Having said this, it somehow does not surprise me that in the aftermath of the events of 9/11 (in the US), many began to turn to God, perhaps as a pillar to succor one in time of need. Should we be using God at our own whims and fancies—we're with Him when times are bad and dismiss Him when it gets better? On that day, God suddenly came into the picture and unity loomed as a mighty fortress in the sight of many. After all, who's going to pick up the pieces when life seems bleak? But for how long does such an amicable spirit last?

On 9/11, did God dial 911? Does God dial 911 for tragic events? Does God involve himself with the affairs of mankind? Does humanity need a resounding wake up call—one that heightens the apprehension of the alarm of utter doom? In the midst of a distressed world can one really have a peace of mind?

And who would have thought that we would come to such a time as this? A time, no doubt, of technological advancement, but also colored by an age of perplexity and daunting catastrophe; a time when airplanes are flying into buildings, towers are crashing and tumbling like dominoes, political unrest, war, prejudice and hatred are on the rise; trains are exploding, upheavals of all sorts are gnawing their tongues for pain, and lives are being hushed in an unprecedented fashion that seems to be the order of the day. Men and women's hearts are becoming enfeebled with fear for what's happening on the earth. And people just aren't so sure which direction to turn.

As I ponder on the reality of the scene and the implications for living, it seems to me that humanity must consciously decide to continue to exist in a world that is filled with pain, and more questions than answers. Though the events of September 11 occurred around a half decade ago, the western world, to say the least, seems to be living in a type of new world order. The world itself felt a shaking, or revolution. Among other things, the reverberation of this shaking has precipitated financial disruptions, homeland security issues, moral considerations, and spiritual effects.

In America, as well as other parts of the globe, this meant that some were eager to find out what on earth is going on! Others might perhaps evaluate the events as a fulfillment of the signs of the time. Either way you cut it, ontologically speaking, it remains the task of humans to seek to confront, if not root out, whatever it is that seems to undermine their existence. For some that means looking deeper within themselves to find the energy to thwart the disasters of life; and for others it implies looking to a power outside of themselves to grab a hold of, or to continue to find consolation in.

With this in mind, what does the mix of global/personal suffering, gargantuan cataclysms,

9/11, constant animosity and apathy in regions such as the Middle East, civil war and unrelenting tyranny in various nations of the world, ethnic hatred and its activities the world over, and human brutality and selfishness mean to you? The cankerous nature of this planet creates such a foul smell in the atmosphere that it appears as if nature itself cries out—"let's get out of here!" Tsunamis, earthquakes, and unprecedented debacles seem to be sensitizing some to the idea that earth is on a headlong path towards stupendous crises.

Mankind, in the meanwhile, takes pleasure in continual perniciousness. Have you viewed or listened to the news recently? I don't know if it's just me, but I have to surmise that the only good thing about the news is that the news hour has ended.

Both society and nature languish and lament bitterly in one voice, as humans continue to look at each other with hatred and suspicion. Nationalism seems to be growing rigid, and even democracy gives the impression of perennial deterioration. In every corner of the habitable globe, the handwriting on the wall seems to be—"What a sorry life." Humanity looks on with grim eyes, as solidarity and human relations tear at the very atmosphere with a vicious claw of pride and calumny. The distress of nations continues to flounder around in a tense struggle that seems to be squeezing mankind by the throat. And people are looking for meaning in the midst of all the mayhem.

How much more gloom and heartache can the human race face? In addition to human degeneration comes the idea of segregation and class. Are you tired of the 'who's black, who's white, who's yellow' theme of the world? Or the secular scheme of identifying persons by background and highest educational achievement? Is it your God-given duty to think of another human as inferior to you—whether it's socially, nationally, or racially?

Modern institutions seem hard pressed for a way to adequately address all these issues. In one sense, however, these concerns are being indirectly and passively dealt with, as the global community is more readily accessible, with a higher rate of inter-cultural correspondence today. But as societies and individuals continue to look at their past and present, constant patterns of suffering, woe, and depravity seem to paint an indelible impression.

Do you think the world of Christ in the first century was any different? His words, given over two millennia ago, seem to reverberate with a vivid echo: "And because iniquity shall abound, the love of many shall wax cold" (Matt. 24:12). And so today, people just don't care. It's about, seeing who can make a better name for themselves first; forget my neighbor! You exist in a world that lies in the middle of a clutter and you begin to wonder, how can change come about? We take up this discussion as we continue on a course of gaping introspection.

The Post-9/11 World

Observation: Since 9/11, humanity has been living in a whole new world. While natural catastrophes continue to abound alongside human endeavor, man-made horrors tell the story of urgent plea. And based on a terse survey I carried out, more people seem to actually think that the world has taken a turn for the worse.

5   When Tragedy Strikes

*I*n the aftermath of 9/11, the social nerve of the world was stimulated, while natural and man-led disasters bombarded humanity's vigor. But what about when tragedy grips the human spirit? We visit now a couple of natural, devastating events marking the opening years of the 21st century.

The loud roar of the sea, or tsunami on December 26, 2004, in the Indian Ocean, left nothing but rubble and broken bodies in its path. It seemed to have not only severed the physical limbs of its victims, but took lives at random and in copious amounts. What seemed to us as the fury of the sea and earth unleashed, left men, women and children not only without a home and family, but it seemed to have also demoralized a nation in the process.

With a death and missing person toll at over hundreds of thousands as we are told, the great tsunami of December 2004, no doubt, left an indelible impression upon the hearts of people everywhere; a time of undeniable anguish. The intensity of the catastrophe seemed so severe, that for many, hope itself seemed to have vanished from the earth in one rapid moment. However, I understand that through such aggressive catastrophes, scientists are beginning to reevaluate their fundamental evolutionistic presuppositions and seriously consider the hand of God in human life.

Then came the insidious monster—Hurricane Katrina, right about high hurricane season—Monday, August 29th, 2005. This Category 5 storm scourged the US Gulf Coast at winds of about 165 miles an hour, with a surge of 29 feet—"the highest ever recorded."[6] This most devastating tragedy and deluge humbled not only sea and land, but it left everything in its path soaking wet and useless. Bodies, power lines, oil lines, residential and business districts were all rendered powerless, as they lay in a hodgepodge of utter chaos. Ranking, perhaps, # 1 in US natural disaster history, "A hurricane like Katrina packs the energy of a 10-megaton nuclear bomb exploding every 20 minutes."[7]

This mixture of storm plus flooding touched on some six states in the Southern United States, sinking many parts in rubble and utter turmoil. New Orleans, which received an imperial blow from the disaster, had a levee system (a protective device against flooding) built to stand against a Category 3 hurricane. But on the dawn of that fateful day, Katrina hit New Orleans as a Category

4 hurricane, with winds that scaled to 140 miles an hour.[8] On September 15, 2005, over 700 people were reported dead and about one million or more persons displaced. The morning after the storm, someone would exclaim, "my Lord, what a morning!"

Pandemonium and disunity of relief coordination broke out in some places as we are told, while some survivors attempted desperately to scramble whatever few pieces of their lives were left. Besides all the anarchy and blame game, for around four to five days storm victims apparently felt they were left to die. Whether it was inside a building, under flood waters, or on the roof top, people were writhing in agony for not only lack of drinking water and food, but also a lack of emotional and moral stability.

Less than a month (aprox. 24 days) after Katrina, just as residents from the Gulf Region thought that they would find fulfillment in a repatriation process, gloom was on the way once more. The exodus of millions of people just in the Houston, Texas area, in preparation for Hurricane Rita, was on the way. Rita was coming in at around 120 miles an hour, reinforcing the fears, frustrations, and devastating claims left by Katrina. It seems as if the US Gulf Region was at once plagued with a terrible hand of calumny and brutal pillage. I have the premonition, though, that Katrina may be the beginning of things to come.

How then, does one pick up the pieces in life when all is shattered in one blast, or as one might put it, in a tempest of utter anguish? This avows the fragility and instability that underscores our human finiteness. Do you know what tomorrow will bring?

Though many often tend to think of themselves as being secure, whatever that may mean, the world around them could collapse at any moment. After all, human life, as it turns out, is not substantiated by materialism, intellectualism, or egocentrism. This helps to turn a fresh page of courage for those dying in despair. Think of it this way—we all are humans, going downstream in the same boat; and there's no way one can exist if there's no one else around. That ultimately translates to a need for a higher power. And if you dare think you can make it alone in this trying world all in your own virtue, then answer this—where will you be tomorrow?

Through all the affliction and mishaps of life, many seek some sort of resolution. Social operations move on, but many just get caught up in whatever wind that blows. Hence the spotlight of the next chapter, as we seek to grapple with the challenge of, not so much modern living, as much as the prevalency of human restlessness.

6   The Da Vinci Awakening

$\mathcal{T}$he milieu of Katrina brought with it a barrage of discontent. Afterwards, some started to ask more questions about the efficacy of social agencies, as it relates to the strain of socio-economic conditions. Inflation, and the constant rise and fluctuation in oil/gas prices weren't doing much to lighten the mood either. All this seemed to have aroused a sense of bewilderment in American consciousness, as commotion gave way to sheer pity and resentment.

For many, the challenge of living in the modern world suddenly blazed into focus. And with that comes the realization—what is life if there's nothing stimulating social awareness and activity? It is in such moods that the restlessness of humanity echoes across the pages of time. Hence, it's not surprising that with the coming of any new fad, so to speak on the market, people will certainly take up the beat and tag along with eager anticipation. Whether it's a social rights club, revelation, illuminati, new age, new world order, da

Vinci, or secret society code, people will follow. Why?

To approach the question above, one has to come to terms with the realization that a supplied answer abounds in many motives. That underscores the capricious and seeking mentality of human nature. One of the latest social fads sought by many, to be sure, is a grand awakening in the person and works of da Vinci. But who was da Vinci?

This character is also known by his first name, Leonardo. He is presumed to have lived from April 15, 1452—May 2, 1519, and "was an Italian Renaissance architect, musician, anatomist, inventor, engineer, geometer and painter."[9] Allegedly, Leonardo is also the twenty-second grand master (out of thirty-nine) of a secret society some believe actually existed—the Priory of Sion, supposedly rising up in the eleventh century.

As the story goes, this secret society (POS—Priory of Sion) was founded by a French royal line in medieval times to preserve the veracity and historical significance of its bloodline. In a Newsweek article, however, it is postulated that, "The Priory was a small group created in 1956 by Pierre Plantard-once convicted of fraud-who fabricated its history."[10]

Some entertain the idea, though, that Mary Magdalene of the gospel story, was in some way connected to the bloodline spoken of above. If that alone was the case, the bloodline probably would not have made much gossip today; except that such a connection was coupled with the fancied notion that Mary, upon fleeing the Holy land, was bearing the daughter of Jesus when she arrived in Gaul (or modern-day France). And the name of the daughter as you might guess is, Sarah—meaning, princess. The inkling of such an intimate relationship between Jesus and Mary Magdalene seems to be influenced, however, by extractions and interpolations into the noncanonical gospel of Philip.

Thus, Mary Madgalene became embroiled with legends and myths which in their own way evolved into a sort of romanticism. Hence the reason for the capricious view of the Holy Grail, which some believe to be the vessel of Christ used at the Last Supper, but epitomized in Mary Magdalene, being the actual vessel bearing significant content. That I do not intend to go into an in-depth discourse on Mary Magdalene, should be met with the consideration—one has to take into account that medieval views about the Magdalene vary widely, based on which European tradition the story is filtered through, from her demonization to her canonization.

And though da Vinci, himself, lived in the time of a rebirth, or renewed interest in the classical age and literature, between the fifteenth and sixteenth centuries, there appears to be a unique attraction to his work in modern times. To place da Vinci in a more immediate context, it is ascertained that he lived in a time when the church, or medieval papacy was dwindling in strength, and the grip on the masses was slowly slipping away. The popes at that time, however, enmeshed themselves in becoming patrons of the arts.

That is also the precise moment in history when Christendom (in this sense, referring to the Middle Ages when the idea of inseparability of state and church reigned supreme) was met with the rising challenge of Protestantism. Thus, particularly in the early sixteenth century, the church (Roman Catholicism) met with able opposition from European states such as Germany and England. It is in that same era that the German priest, Martin Luther, becoming more recognized during the final days of da Vinci, would become a bitter thorn in the flesh of the Papal See.

Leonardo also seems to have drawn the attention of many not only to his life and work of art, but to his personal mirrored writings as well. It is believed that such writings may have been linked to his new anatomy and engineering ideas, or to his work in general, which in his time was supposedly transported by way of cryptex handling, in order to keep his messages private. Leonardo, however, became famous, in part, for two specific works of art—*The Last Supper* and *Mona Lisa*. The *Mona Lisa,* in particular, is held to be perhaps the most famous painting in history and is romanticized by many. The painting itself has become quite renowned because it is believed to have been fused with an enigmatic smile, which gives onlookers reason to ponder on the meaning.

Preachers across America have also taken interest in Leonardo's work. In that regard, some have even done mini series at their churches, as they turn their attention to the theme of hidden codes, secret societies and erroneous doctrines, as it pertains to Biblical teaching and spiritual welfare.

This can be seen as an attempt to dissipate impressions, or to inform the congregation about sentiments which seek to undermine the gospel of Christ, as recorded in the New Testament. But people are realizing that the rebirth in interest in da Vinci's symbolism, or code will come and go just like other fads in history.

7 Facing the 21st Century

*N*ow, human restlessness rolls on in high-tech society, and today's fast-paced life advances with harsh demands to keep up. The rush is on. And besides that, the twenty-first century lingers in a world that has apparently taken a one-way ride to destination—*Insensitivity*. Thus, many seek recourse from an impersonal world that seems to function somewhat like an accordion. It brings people and cultures together, then pushes them further apart.

Granted, many eagerly forecasted some sort of grand, mystical ushering in of this millennium; and many more looked forward to a beaming century of harmony and change. But somehow all the swelling anticipation seemed to have died, when the opening months of the twenty-first century came and went as if nothing had happened. You are now among those living in the stir of the post-9/11 world, and surrounded by the exasperation faced by humanity. And human flagitiousness, greed and degeneration seem to be top factors that will shape the rest of the twenty-first century.

Even though political, environmental, nuclear, technological and social science all tell us something of the future of government and society, they still seem ill-equipped to adequately handle intercultural and international antagonism. Should we then as a human race all compete to tear each other apart, or realize that we are all, in some way, connected to each other?

Whether you recognize it or not, the present is breeding calamity for the future. And based on current socio-political trends, I do not sense a better world of peace in the foreseeable future. Even if governments and social movements forecast a better world of change, progress, prosperity and peace, it appears as though everyone is ignoring the world of now. Humans must rise to the challenge of being alienated from one another.

While catastrophes and social problems continue to underscore the plight of the human condition, humanity seeks a way to maintain a face of courage. And then there's the bigger issue of where are we going? As people grapple with the notion of being independent of God, the tension within the human spirit rises.

The burst of technology today calls into account the coming together of the global community, but even that in itself isn't sufficient in addressing human restlessness. Humans recognize their need for God, but today the world seems to be diametrically opposed to the idea as if to say, "we can do it alone." Well, whether you like it or not, God will reign and will not remain silent. In fact, He is the one still holding the universe and the fragments of planet earth together, in spite of humanity's erratic and self-seeking ways.

I'm not sure what you think of when you think of God; but when I consider His grandeur, or as one may put it, His immensity, I recognize mercy, love, peace, and I will never forget *grace*.

Grace so awesome and so free
That reaches down to quicken me
  Oh how I long to keep that trace
  To tell the triumph of God's grace

C.L.H.

Natural selection has done nothing for me, for it could never design purpose for my life. Macro-evolutionary data, agnosticism and humanistic idealism, all blend to obliterate the idea of a need for God. But the more self-sufficient mankind becomes, the less the import of a relationship with God is deemed worthy. In the end this leads to an attitude of carelessness, indifference and self-indulgence, which in itself becomes the venom that ends in self-annihilation.

And here we are, standing no longer on the threshold of a distinct and new day, but living the realities of a new millennium. Yet, it seems to be the same old story; wars, rumors of wars, and an unceasing string of social violence, restlessness, tension and immorality. In fact, even while I am writing this book, the pangs of warfare are in the air. One of the major current highlights, concerns the fighting between Israel and Hezbollah—a militant group with operations within Southern Lebanon, and close to the border of Northern Israel. And even as I am closing this very paragraph, countries such as France and America are in the process of evacuating tens of thousands of their citizens out of Lebanon by air, sea and land.

Today's society craves something more, realizing that throughout time the attempts by men and women to meld cultures and bring the human race into harmony, have only proved futile.

As it was in the days of the first century A.D., so it is today. From the Great Wall of China to the prodigious hills of the Americas, men and women continue to contrive schemes to defeat each other, in more ways than one. The aura of the human condition seems to suggest that humanity has lapsed into a chronic mode of belligerence and indifference.

And what's the point? We hate and kill each other till we're tired of it? Or simply seek to undermine each other for the heck of it? With all the peace talks of the last century, and the political summits that have met to analyze global, social stability, the twenty-first century has still not been inoculated against warfare, sadism, greed, starvation, and ethnic hatred.

This should be no surprise because people are becoming accustomed to sudden destruction, every time the cry for peace and safety is heralded. But one day, God himself will wipe away the very last tear drop (Rev. 21:4). The last tears will fall and the last streak of pain will writhe in agony, as it sings its final song. Ah but one day the last battle cry must be heard! The last infantry will march; the last gun will fire. One day the last soldier will fight; the last victim will fall, and the last grave must be dug. Then one day, the final taint of anguish and sorrow must wave goodbye.

But until then we must carry on. Until then, we can approach the storms of life with courage, or wail in despair. We can rise up with renewed vigor in our step, or sit still in a cesspool of wretchedness and drink from the cup of dejection, while we eat the bread of dismay. Until then, we need to bear in mind as individuals, that as long as we have the ability to reason, there's no such thing as being immune to the world around us. On that token, may the people of earth rise up; take a good look at the person next to you, and determine whether or not he/she is important just as you are. Today then, people must decide their part in social indifference, and by extension global conflict, realizing that we're all members of the same family.

Endnotes

1. Bruce L. Shelley. *Church History In Plain Language.* Texas: Word Books Publisher, 1982.

2. Ibid.

3. Source: *American Heritage Dictionary,* Fourth Edition, Topic: "Islam."

4. Matthew S. Gordon, *Islam* (New York: Facts On File, 1991), 12.

5. http://dictionary.reference.com/browse/Islam. Retrieved: 7/06/06.

6. The Lost City, *Newsweek Online* (2005, September 12). From site: msnbc.msn.com.

7. Ibid.

8. Ibid.

9. http://www.reference.com/browse/wiki/ Leonardo_da_Vinci. Retrieved 5/18/06.

10. An Inconvenient Woman, *Newsweek,* May 29, 2006.

978-0-595-40997-6
0-595-40997-0